The Art of
Flower Arrangement

THE ART OF

Flower Arrangement

by

TATSUO ISHIMOTO

*

CROWN PUBLISHERS
New York, N.Y.

FOR ELDRED AND AZZIE IRELAND

Table of Contents

Foreword

If there is one *natural* art it is flower arrangement. Consider the materials you have at hand: flowers themselves, in endless variety, as well as all other green and growing things; color, from nature's own vivid palette; textures, shapes, delicate or vigorous; wood, bark, branches, stones. In a flower composition you can express the growth plans of nature herself. You can heighten the beauty of your materials, and you can have a wonderful time doing it.

Most books on flower arrangement are based on the classical Japanese approach. They interpret the various traditional Japanese schools of arrangement: the *Ikenobo,* the *Senkei Ryu* and others. They talk of secondary and tertiary development, of intersecting planes and bilateral symmetry. The whole thing is discussed on a very high level. It is beautiful and perfectly sound, but to the average American flower lover it is about as clear as a treatise on differential calculus.

In Japan, for centuries, the arrangement of flowers has been considered one of the highest of social arts. The subject, over the years, has become meshed in tradition, hemmed in with strict rules that brook little deviation. It is true that in comparatively recent times a modern school of flower arrangement, the *Moribana,* has arisen in Japan; but even this style has its rules and restrictions.

Japanese results in flower arrangement are often indescribably beautiful. Many of the arrangements in this book are based on Japanese principles, but just as many are not. Nature herself is a notorious rule-breaker; perhaps we may be excused if we follow her example.

The severity of most classical arrangements, the restricted use of color, run counter to American custom and taste. Principles of design and technique we will discuss at length, but informally, and there will be no rules!

T. I.

CANNONDALE, CONNECTICUT.

Your own Approach
to Flowers

It's important and satisfying to
bring nature inside your home...

Millions of Americans think dogs are important, and enjoy having them live indoors with the family. Very few Americans would consider building a new home that didn't have at least one picture window, framing a natural view. Dogs and picture windows — both are expressions of a healthy national desire to live more closely with nature.

Today modern architecture is urging us in that direction. One man builds a house over a waterfall. Another has his house built to enclose a giant oak tree. A third has a natural stone outcropping as one wall of his living room. Frank Lloyd Wright for years has oriented his houses to the surrounding land, placing windows and wall openings where each will frame a natural outdoor picture.

At the same time modern interior design urges us toward simplicity, plain walls and ceilings in natural materials, uncluttered rooms, a feeling of space and freedom, an escape from boxed-in unnatural restrictions.

The growing interest in flower arrangement supports this trend. Not only do today's interiors provide a wonderful background for flowers, but flowers and greens displayed indoors help satisfy the fundamental desires to live closely with nature and to enjoy natural beauty.

Study flowers in a garden...

The place to begin your serious study of flower arrangement is out-of-doors, almost anywhere out-of-doors. Walk in the woods to observe the way plants and bushes and trees grow. Notice the way flowers grow in a garden. Here is nature making

This is unnatural and exaggerated, of course. But placing flowers in a vase and scattering them a little is not flower arrangement.

This is natural. The flowers are secured in a flower holder, as they were secured a short time ago in the ground.

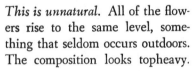

This is unnatural. All of the flowers rise to the same level, something that seldom occurs outdoors.
The composition looks topheavy.

This is natural. Stems are cut
carefully to permit each flower to
rise to its own level. The composition has balance and unity.

her own arrangements (with some help from the gardener who planned the color
and flower combinations!). In many flowers big blooms mass at the base, with
smaller blooms above and fresh buds nodding at the very top. Notice how the most
pleasant effects often come when like flowers rise, one above another, step ladder
fashion. Notice the unstudied informality of flower growth. Watch for isolated
floral effects that excite and please you.

Almost any natural growing flower composition that you find in a garden can be the
inspiration of a flower arrangement inside your home. Usually you can heighten
and intensify this effect by eliminating all confusing or intruding elements, con-
centrating on the central idea. If you keep your imagination alert to the natural
suggestions offered in your garden, you will be on your way toward a flower arrangement style all your own.

Some principles of design...

Hard and fast rules are one thing, principles of good design another. You need follow no set rules in making your flower compositions, but you will want to work within the broad limits of good design, limits set clearly before you in the growing plan of flowers themselves.

You will want your flower compositions to have *harmony*. That means, simply, that all of the parts should go well together. Often you can achieve harmony by repeating, within your arrangement, colors, shapes or numbers, leaves and flowers in pairs or threes. You will see many examples of this kind of harmony in arrangements later in the book.

You will want your composition to be in *balance*. Sometimes they will balance formally, or symmetrically (pages 43, 47, 73), flowers and leaves of equal height and weight on either side. More often they will balance informally or asymetrically. In achieving informal balance (pages 35, 54, 120), you will have to follow your own sense of what is right, working for a horizontal or slanting line that is just long enough, with a mass just heavy enough, to balance your vertical line. A good visual sense of balance will come with practice.

The first time you make an arrangement that contains both leaves and flowers, you will establish simple color *contrast*. Later you will include two or more flower types in your arrangements. You will learn to work with many kinds of contrast — color (including the color of your container and of the background), shape, line and form. In all cases your objective will be a pleasing whole, an over-all effect. Your experiments with contrast will do much to help you to develop an original style of your own. Your own visual judgment is your best guide in color selections. Remember that colors close together in the color scale go well together — blue with purple and violet; orange with yellow and green. White goes well with almost all colors, particularly the darker hues — red, blue and purple.

Arrangements using many different flowers, or many different colors of the same flower, are often unwise. The effect is more apt to be dizzying than pleasing. Two different flowers, or three, are usually enough, in two or three colors.

One basic principle of design occurs regularly in nature, and in most good flower compositions — the idea of *dominance*, of having one part of your arrangement dominate the whole. This central dominating feature captures the attention of any observer; other parts of the composition support it.

Containers come first. You don't need very many, but they should be the right kind...

Flowers can look well in almost anything — a fifteenth century porcelain bowl or a dime store baking dish — provided that the shape and size and color of the container are suited to your arrangement.

Almost all of the arrangements made for this book use one or another of the four basic containers shown above. All are simple glazed pottery, white or pastel in color. Two are shallow, two deep. The four represent just about all the variety you will need to reproduce successfully the arrangements discussed here.

But does that mean you should throw out, or never use, the vases you have now? Not at all — the more you have the better. You'll find frequent use for every one of your containers, except possibly the very narrow-necked vases. Bowls or dishes, wide-topped containers, give you much more freedom in arrangement, and your flowers last longer — the generous opening lets in air to refresh them.

Much of the fun in flower arrangement can come with your own discovery of new containers — floral uses for the everyday pots, kettles, bowls and dishes that you have around the house. On the opposite page is a typical household collection: the favorite old bean pot, a wooden bucket, a pottery pitcher and a copper pitcher (fine for leaves or evergreens), an old copper teapot, a heavy pottery coffee cup. The low small dishes are perfect for short-stemmed garden flowers (dwarf marigolds, pansies, or small zinnias and petunias). The collection here simply suggests the sorts of container that can easily be pressed into service. You'll soon make your own discoveries, in your own kitchen and china cupboard, or in the dusty corners of your attic and basement.

Remember that containers, important as they are, must not steal the show from the flowers or greens they support. Often, for this reason, a humble self-effacing bowl plays a more effective part in a flower composition than the most handsome piece of fine pottery.

As a rule, containers should be neutral or soft in color, presenting a quieter appearance than the flowers above. The bowls and dishes used throughout this book were chosen deliberately to emphasize this point. For the most part, they are simple pottery pieces, off-white or soft pastel in color.

Make sure that the vases and other containers you use are spotlessly clean. Even a small amount of grease and dirt can affect the water and shorten the life of your flowers.

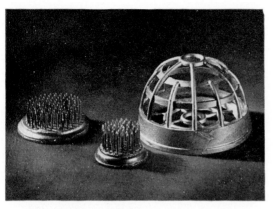

You will need needle and wire holders

Lay in a supply of modeling clay

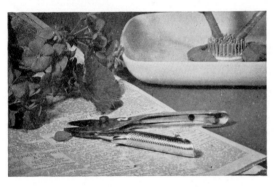

Get a pair of sharp flower shears

Collect a few beautiful stones

Tools are few, but important...

Like all hobbies, flower arrangement requires some special paraphernalia of its own, but far less than most. The chances are that you have now most or all of the containers you will need. The rest is easy.

Holders come first. There are a great many kinds in the shops, but you will get along quite well with just two — needle holders and wire holders. Needle holders come in many shapes — round, oval, rectangular and half-moon. They should be heavy. You will probably want several in different sizes. Wire holders are particularly good for the heavier-stemmed flowers. One or two will most likely take care of your needs at first.

But holders in themselves are not enough. You will want your arrangements to be securely fixed, and even the best weighted holder can topple over and spoil your careful flower composition if it is left unsecured.

Modeling clay is the answer. You can get a supply at many florist shops, and at any art supply store. Use small bits at intervals along the sides of your holder, pressing the clay and holder firmly against the bottom of the bowl. A very small holder, if well secured with clay, can support surprisingly heavy branches, stems and flowers.

The container should be clean and perfectly dry before you fix the holder in position. Clay grips best on a dry surface. It may come loose if applied when the bowl is wet. The clay itself should also be dry.

Next you will want to start a collection of stones. Keep the small ones in a glass coffee jar, the large ones on a shelf with your other flower equipment.

Look for rounded stones, two to six inches across, mottled in color or veined. Try to find one or two in the soft earth colors: brown, yellow, beige and brick red. Next get some small flat, round and oval pebbles, white and gray and black. Keep an eye out for some rough angular granite pieces. These are suggestions — you will enjoy making your own finds.

A sharp cutting tool is the one other piece of really essential equipment. Flower shears are best, but a very sharp knife will do. Many flower experts frown on scissors, but even scissors are all right if you can set aside a good extra-sharp pair exclusively for flower cutting.

Sharpness can't be over-emphasized — a good, clean cut, bruising and pinching the stem as little as possible, permits greater absorption of water, and so insures a longer life for your flowers.

Now — how much flower equipment must you have? Not so very much: a few basic containers, a half-dozen holders, some stones, a little clay, and a pair of flower shears. Can you spare these few essentials a shelf or cupboard to themselves? If you can, good — you will work more easily if all your supplies are readily at hand.

Some flower hobbyists prefer to make their compositions in the kitchen or flower room (if they are lucky enough to have a spare room just for flowers), then carry them to the chosen place of display. However, arrangements made on the spot — that is, where they are to be displayed — are far more satisfactory.

You might try collecting your flower tools in a portable box so you can easily make your arrangements in their intended surroundings. Doing so, you will find yourself composing the flowers in harmony with the walls and furniture, always having in mind where the arrangement's audience will be seated or standing.

If you can sketch, even crudely, you will find it a help to rough out the general plan for your arrangement before you start. Even if you can't draw a line, have your plan in mind first, considering the location in the room, the lighting, the colors and your flower materials.

Cut flowers will last much longer
if you treat them carefully...

If you pick your own flowers, do it in the early morning before the sun is high, or pick them after sundown. Sunshine closes the pores of flowers — you want the pores open, so that the stems can absorb water easily. Cut the stems slantwise to increase the water-absorbing area. Make as sharp a cut as possible.

When you come indoors, plunge the flower stems in deep water. Leave them there for several hours, if you can, before arranging them. Keep your flowers in a humid room, in the dark or at least not in direct sunshine. Fresh air will help your flowers last, but heat hastens their withering. The coldest room in your house is the best place for your flowers. Never should you place them near hot radiators, or in currents of hot air.

Cut away all foliage and leaves that will extend below water level in your arrangement. If these greens decompose they will pollute the water. Re-cut stems and change water regularly, daily if possible. If you make a slanting cut, the stems can not rest squarely on the bottom of the container and so shut off their air supply.

There are many methods you can use to increase the water absorption of your flowers. Boiling is one good method, particularly effective with dahlias and poppies. Plunge the stem ends into boiling water for a minute or two (protecting the flowers from the steam), then into cold water. The boiling water will have opened the pores.

Burning the stems over an open burner also opens the pores. Or you can crush and slit the stem ends: this is a particularly good method for plants with heavy, woody stems. Branches can often take a two-inch cut up the stems before you place them in water.

Frequently you can revive wilting flowers if you act in time. Shorten the stems with sharp-angled cuts and place in deep water. Store in a cool darkened room overnight.

Often you can achieve beautiful arrangements with plant material already withered. Part of the effectiveness of the arrangement above is in the bare expanse of old wood of the hydrangea. Note the old flower head at the left which picks up the color and quality of the bared stems.

Flowers can "wake up" every
room in your house...

Flowers belong all through a house, in the kitchen just as much as the living room, on your bedside table as well as your dining room table. The color and naturalness of flowers immediately wake up a room, warm it, introduce the kind of live beauty that everyone needs and appreciates.

Entrance hall — Notice how three branches of fuchsia add life and beauty to their otherwise rigid surroundings.

Dining room   Sun room

Living room   Bedroom

If you don't have your own garden...

If you are one of the lucky ones, if you have your own luxurious beds of tulips and poppies, your own roses and daffodils, if you have splashy color in your garden from May to October, then this page is not for you.

But for every flower lover who can grow all the flowers she needs, there are many who cannot. Apartment dwellers, particularly, must know their way around the florist shops, know which flowers will make a good showing for a dollar or two, which will last and which won't.

On the next three pages are a few of the many flowers that are almost always good buys in season, and which you can easily dramatize in your own arrangements. Each of them appears in an arrangement of its own, later in the book. Most are old favorites, annuals and perennials that every gardener knows and loves well.

The selection is arbitrary — no two flower lovers are likely to agree on any dozen flowers, and no two readers are likely to agree completely with this selection. But remember, these flowers are not recommended for the gardener who can grow what she likes, but for the garden-less flower lover who must buy what she can afford.

French Marigolds are among the hardiest of cut flowers, and are inexpensive.

Double Shasta daisies last a long time — and they are extremely easy to arrange.

Zinnia, a favorite annual, lasts well and is inexpensive. Comes in various colors.

Snapdragon, various colors. Fine for both horizontal and vertical arrangements.

Marguerite, white and yellow. Showy, inexpensive and very easy to arrange.

Chrysanthemum, all sizes and many colors. Another good late season buy.

Gaillardia, maroon and bronze. Often a good buy until very late in the season.

Strawflower, good as "everlasting" for winter arrangements. Colors are various.

Sweet Pea, handsome for table bouquets. Comes in variety of fresh pastel colors.

Coreopsis, a cheerful yellow perennial, makes beautiful informal compositions.

Iris, many varieties, in every possible shade. If you love color, you'll love Iris.

Dahlia, small pompom and ball types, large decorative types. Many colors.

Carnation, white, pink and red. A good buy during mid-summer, easy to arrange.

Calendula, yellow, orange. Usually one of the best buys at the florists' shops.

Seventy-eight Arrangements
You Can Try for Yourself...

A discussion of design and design principles, of balance, rhythm, contrast and harmony, is all very well, but a demonstration of these principles is much more useful.

The flower arrangements on the following pages constitute such a demonstration. Each arrangement presents one or more fundamental principles. Taken together, the group of arrangements explores most of the problems you will meet in your work with flowers.

Almost all of the flowers used here are readily available in florist shops across the country. Most of them are gardener's favorites, and inexpensive, as well.

You can make any of these arrangements with a variety of flowers. If you don't have, or can't buy, small pompom dahlias, try marigolds or zinnias instead. Substitute iris for gladioli, snapdragon for larkspur. Whenever you develop a particularly successful composition, try variations with other, quite different flowers. Remember, this is the freest, least restricted art there is. Don't worry about breaking the "rules". Self-expression is what counts, and creative effort offers its own very special rewards.

Don't be afraid to vary
the length of the stems

In both of the arrangements below five shasta daisies rise from a single needle holder. On the left the daisies are arranged as they come from the florist or garden, all of the stems uniform in length. The result is awkward, top-heavy, unnatural.

But what a difference it makes when each stem is cut at a different point . . . the whole arrangement following the natural curves of the strongest highest bloom. In this way five flowers come together into a single exciting composition.

(Picture to left) Even if you have a dozen or so daisies don't hesitate to try the same vertical rising arrangement. Here eleven flowers are placed in 3-4-2-2 order, yet no two blooms are on quite the same level. The result is a *free* composition — garden naturalness in a pottery bowl.

Theme and variations: more "growing" arrangements using short and long stems...

A beginner in flower composition does well to limit herself to one *color* and one *kind* of flower at first. Here are three interesting practice arrangements, built up with ten, thirteen and fourteen double Shasta daisies, each designed to achieve a natural growing effect.

The Shasta, one of the hardiest of the perennials, takes well to cutting — it will last and last if treated carefully.

You can use a single needle holder in making these arrangements. Place the longest single flower first, then measure each succeeding bloom against it, cut, and fix into position.

In the arrangement on the left above, six flowers rise vertically from the bowl; seven additional flowers float on the surface of the water, concealing the holder. In the arrangement on the right and on the opposite page, the lowest blooms are placed to conceal the holder.

A free arrangement...

Much of the pleasure in flower arrangement comes in making your own "free" compositions. There is a special satisfaction in recreating the unstudied informality of nature herself, in a corner of your own living room.

The arrangement above uses a six-inch bowl, with one needle holder to support thirteen yellow marguerites. The flowers face out in three directions from the wall, with stems cut to suggest the continuous upward movement of natural growth. The result is a flower composition which is different from every angle — one that will still surprise and interest you, no matter how many times you study it.

A massed arrangement...

This table bouquet contains two dozen yellow marguerites rising from a wire mesh holder in a small four-inch bowl. The center blooms are placed first to establish the over-all height. In making massed bouquets, height in relation to the bowl is im-portant. If you let your flowers rise at least one and one-half times the height of the bowl, you won't be far off.

Measure each flower carefully before placing and cutting. Build up the arrangement bloom by bloom. Arrange the skeleton first; then fill in open spaces. To avoid an uninteresting "painfully symmetrical" appearance vary stem-lengths slightly, and let three or four individual flowers face outward and downward from the bowl's rim.

It's not how many you have;
it's what you do with them...

A surprising number of people have still to make one pleasant discovery in flower arrangement — the unimportance of numbers.

It's wonderful to have flowers in profusion, dozens and dozens of them, but not at all a necessary requirement in making exciting (or impressive) arrangements.

The whole fun of arranging flowers centers in making the composition, and there's no satisfaction quite like that which comes from creating a stimulating flower picture with three blooms, or even one. For example —

Here is an arrangement
using just *one* gladiola...

This is a vertical arrangement, one yellow gladiola stalk with five gladioli leaves. The leaves have been placed to accentuate the strong vertical line of the central flower. The leaves are cut in successively shorter lengths and inserted with the gladiola in a single needle holder.

1. Establish the dimensions of the finished arrangement with first blooms placed.

Just as in baking a cake, work according to a *plan...*

Many flower lovers who are good with a pencil sketch their arrangements first. This isn't really necessary, but it does suggest the importance of having your finished composition clearly in mind before you start. First — what do you want it to look like? And then, how shall you bring it about?

The arrangement here, which might be called informal balance, is similar to the cantilever principle used in architecture and bridge building. The longest chrysanthemums, extending to the right beyond the bowl, are supported by the heavier mass rising vertically and to the left.

The skeleton of the arrangement, once clearly in mind, can be established with the first few blooms placed. The arrangement is made with small chrysanthemums about one inch in diameter, gold with orange-red centers. The pottery vase measures six by twelve inches; it is white outside, pale yellow within. Support comes from a single wire holder.

2. Fill in carefully, one flower at a time, working along the crest of the arrangement.

3. With the crest complete, begin placement of shorter-stemmed blooms on sides.

A vertical arrangement,
in three parts...

Iris or gladioli leaves make excellent materials for you to use in composing formal arrangements.

On the left, six leaves establish the three basic levels, one leaf and one tributary at each level. Notice how all leaves are anchored at the back of the needle holder. On the right the first three flowers are placed at the primary and secondary levels.

On the opposite page the composition is complete. The lowest level flowers face out, partially concealing the holder.

This arrangement rises easily
from a single source...

The source in this case, is a well-secured needle holder. Place the holder one-third of the way along a shallow bowl, and anchor it with clay.

Place the geraniums, then clip to achieve a simple, easily defined line.

Experiment with the lower foliage, trying it until you achieve the right effect, a green mass with single stalks rising above.

Needle holder may be concealed by leaves (above) or by stones (below).

A few will go a long long way...

Here are four arrangements, using three, five, eight and twelve button dahlias. In the first the flowers are cut to reach the traditional three levels . . .

In the second arrangement extra blooms are added above, the primary level being carried alone by the single largest bloom.

In the third arrangement eight dahlias face out from the bowl against a background of dark green leaves.

On the opposite page a full dozen is used . . . a mass rising from the bowl with four single blooms, in two lengths, reaching above.

You have only three . . .

You have five . . .

You have eight — or a dozen ⫸→

Breakfast room or kitchen — a small arrangement makes everything taste better...

Brighten the table with flowers; and any family meal, even a hurried early morning breakfast, becomes an occasion. Such arrangements needn't be pretentious. Almost any colorful flowers will do. But the same principles apply as in more formal table decoration.

Remember that the arrangement will be viewed by people *sitting down*. It should look best from a low level. Sit down yourself when you arrange the flowers, and you'll be sure to avoid mistakes.

Remember to complete the arrangement on all sides — it will not be against a wall, and must be equally attractive from all angles.

Remember finally that people eating together like to see each other. Make yours a *low* arrangement — place your flowers in a shallow bowl and keep the top of the arrangement well below eye level.

Kitchen breakfast: Deep orange gaillardias in a cereal bowl add color and warmth to the kitchen breakfast table.

Family luncheon: Everyone feels better, everything tastes better, when there are flowers with the family luncheon.

This small arrangement (also on luncheon table, opposite page) is made in a low round pottery bowl, with one large wire holder.

Small white chrysanthemums, one inch in diameter, are placed first, setting the height and circumference of the arrangement. A few yellow marigolds, two inches in diameter, are added at intervals

PHLOX

Practice making arrangements
in a low dish or bowl...

If you use a clay-anchored holder, you can escape the limitations that high-sided vases place on flower arrangements. Whether your flowers are long-stemmed or short, as often as not only a low bowl or dish will permit you to create a natural composition.

Above a large needle holder, well anchored, supports a free arrangement of phlox.

On the opposite page a round needle holder, anchored with clay, supports a simple arrangement of iris.

One trick is in the cutting...

Your flower shears are probably your one most important tool in making natural arrangements. Don't be afraid to use them.

Study the way flowers grow outdoors. Notice that the most pleasing effects usually are found when flowers rise one above another, at varying heights, buds at the top, big mature blooms below. These are effects you can easily duplicate with cut flowers, if you can bring yourself to cut some of those beautiful long stems.

Here five deep yellow zinnias are arranged in a ten-inch round pottery dish. Notice how the uniform stem lengths make an unnatural grouping, the individual flowers lost in one mass, the whole composition top-heavy. On the right the same five blooms are rearranged, two blooms together at the base, one bloom rising by itself at the very top. Each single flower plays its part in the over-all composition.

On the opposite page, nine zinnias are grouped in a six-inch gray pottery vase. The flowers rise in threes, in natural unstudied order.

Use the buds to fill in open
spaces in a free arrangement...

Calendulas, like zinnias, are annuals that take well to cutting. Their warm yellow or orange color will bring light into the darkest corners of your living room.

The arrangement on the left uses seven flowers and a few buds, fixed with a single needle holder. The buds are placed carefully to emphasize the upward-growing movement of the arrangement, as well as to bridge open spaces.

Below, calendulas are arranged to overflow a small bowl. Notice how the flowers face upward on the left, face out and down on the right. Again, one needle holder is enough to support the arrangement.

Arrange your *branches* in three levels too...

Flowers, leaves and branches seem to arrange *naturally* in threes. Why this should be so isn't very clear, although the classical Japanese schools of flower arrangement, based entirely on the three "lines," have a rich and colorful symbolism developed through the centuries: the primary level is symbolic of Heaven, the secondary of Man and the tertiary of Earth.

At any rate you will find a rule of three useful as a general guide. Just as the geranium arrangements on pages 62 and 63 were both made with three sprays, so this arrangement of red berries is made with three branches.

Each branch has been trimmed carefully to achieve a severe, sharply-defined line. The longest (primary) branch was placed first, bent slightly to bow out from the bowl. The second and third branches were also slightly bent before placement.

COTONEASTER

An informal arrangement, in thirds...

This arrangement is considerably less severe than the one on the preceding page. Branches which had many small sub-branches were chosen. These, in effect, are tributaries of the three basic lines on which the composition is based. The arrangement is placed in a seven-inch square pottery bowl, anchored with one needle holder.

Or make your own composition...

Sooner or later you will want to compose your own quite original arrangements. Whether you keep to the classical rule of three, or disregard rules completely, stick with it — nothing is so satisfying as your own composition.

The arrangement above, still made with three branches, suggests the fundamental unity present in even the most haphazard natural growth.

A dozen white carnations..

Here is an everyday problem in flower arrangement, one that you probably have faced many times. What can you do with the bare dozen flowers your husband brings home, or a friend sends when you are ill?

1. *You can't do this:* A conventional bouquet takes more than a dozen. This one took twenty-one flowers before it was complete.

2. *You could do this:* Clip the stems at varying lengths and place all twelve in a six-inch colored vase. It looks very neat, if not very exciting.

3. *But why not try this?* Put a needle holder in a square (or round) vase. Fix the two longest-stemmed flowers on the right side. Step five more down the same side, the lowest facing out from the rim of the vase. Then balance the flower column with the remaining five flowers, massed to the left, one single bloom reaching well out from the vase. You've spent an extra five minutes, but what a difference! You have an arrangement that will delight you every time you look at it.

Geraniums are *naturally* informal...

A lot of people make fun of geraniums. That doesn't really matter a bit, because a whole lot *more* people love them tenderly. Geraniums are friendly flowers, naturally informal; and that's the way they should be arranged.

On the left three sprays of purple flowers are arranged in a four-inch bowl, with one needle holder. The thick foliage has been trimmed away to permit a clean-cut, simple composition.

On the right three branches with pink blooms are arranged in a sweeping diagonal movement. Again, excess foliage has been cut away. The branches are anchored in a single needle holder. The bowl is about eight inches in diameter.

Three simple variations...

The delphinium is a wonderful perennial, one that takes well to cutting, a favorite among all of the tall blue and purple flowers.

Here are three delphinium arrangements, two in composition with brilliant orange gaillardia.

On the left purple, blue and lavender blooms rise together from a gray pottery vase. The arrangement uses one small wire holder.

On the right three delphinium sprays and six gaillardia "grow" from a single source, in careful balance.

On the opposite page big gaillardia mask the base of a vertical arrangement, with the high-rising delphinium reaching up and up with smaller and smaller blooms.

Privet with stones...
Two arrangements

The American countryside is a treasure-house of leaves. Whether you live in Connecticut, Wisconsin or California, there is hardly a week in the year that the road-sides don't offer all sorts of exciting raw material for your arrangements.

Leaves, useful as they are in combinations with flowers, deserve arrangements of their own. The wish for "something green in the house" is a wish you can satisfy easily, and in endless variety, if you are lucky enough to have your own garden or live within reach of open country. But even if you are an apartment dweller, your florist is sure to stock a good variety of fresh leaves the year round.

Here are two leaf arrangements you should find easy, and quite effective.

Above an irregular, natural leaf-hedge pushes up from the stones. On the right the leaves sweep upward on one side, balanced by a lower clump on the opposite side of the bowl. The stones can be the anchor, or you can use a holder concealed behind the stones.

Turn nasturtiums to
face their audience...

Here is another of the homely (but popular) annuals that can be surprisingly effective in arrangements.

Nasturtiums, by their nature, have a good side and a bad side. (That's the bad side above.) If you use them for arrangement against a wall, you can then make every

flower and leaf contribute toward the total effect, "good" sides facing out into the room. And don't snub nasturtium leaves. Those flat, green rough-circles are nature's own backdrop, which will emphasize the beauty of the single nasturtium blooms.

The uncrowded arrangement above uses just five flowers, a wire holder and a six-inch bowl.

Let nasturtiums flow away from the bowl...

Nasturtiums are typical home garden flowers. (The ones used here were picked in a friend's back garden in Marin County, California.) They are unpretentious flowers; give them unpretentious treatment.

Here are two nasturtium arrangements, basically similar, made to bring out this flower's natural informality. Nasturtiums are loose and free-flowing in their movement; they struggle against confinement. Don't fight them — let them flow away from the bowl. The results can be delightful.

On the left, the leaves make a central green mass, with one spray escaping; on the right, the flowers, flowing away, balance the dominant leafy arrangement.

Triple contrast — color,
height and form

Here is an arrangement you can make with many different materials — exciting to look at when it is complete, but very easy to put together.

1. Build the background with coprosma — any good straight-stemmed greens you have in your garden or can coax from your florist. Start with a single stalk that sets the height of the arrangement.

2. Here coxcomb is placed next, a few sprays, leaving space for the chrysanthemums to come. The tallest coxcomb stands well below the top of the leafy background.

3. *Opposite page,* the composition complete: three chrysanthemums are placed at the lowest level, two hugging the rim of the bowl. The arrangement here was made with a bowl eight inches square, using two needle holders.

HYDRANGEA with
MARIGOLDS

Simplicity is always a good idea...

Here is a good example of what simplicity can mean in flower arrangement . . . a composition that's sure to bring admiring comment from your guests.

Your materials are three branches of hydrangea, and three yellow-orange marigolds. Anchor the needle holder firmly with modeling clay.

Just five blooms and a few leaves...

Petunias, a favorite among gardeners, can be just as effective indoors as out. Their color range may be limited; but the many varieties offer you a wide selection.

Here five of the double variety sweep upward in a rhythmic right to left movement, which is repeated in the leafy background. You can use either iris or gladioli leaves.

1. Place a wire flower holder in a six-inch pottery bowl.

2. Establish the height and circumference with the first half-dozen blooms.

Sweet Pea bouquet... you build the framework first...

The table bouquet, although hardly a natural form, has always been an American favorite. As in all massed arrangements, a feeling of unity is important — the design should be roughly symmetrical and the flower mass should conform to the height and shape of the bowl you are using.

In this sweet pea bouquet a feeling of profusion, of soft color spilling over the bowl on all sides, is obtained by cutting the longest stems two and one-half times the height of the bowl, and by allowing individual stems to vary from the average lengths.

3. Build up the arrangement carefully, bloom by bloom, from all sides.

4. Measure each flower, and cut individually before placement.

DAHLIAS with MARGUERITES

A small "revolving"
arrangement, to
be viewed from
all sides...

1. Place the dahlias first. Carefully measure each flower's height.

2. Complete the outline with dahlias. Turn the bowl, or walk around it.

3. Add marguerites at intervals at all levels and all sides of the arrangement.

4. Notice how the marguerites break up the otherwise severe hemispherical outline, each one turning upward or outward naturally. The small bowl, seven inches in diameter, contains a wire holder.

Rising from a bed of pebbles...

Here is another arrangement equally effective from front or back. The orange-colored flowers, growing in clusters along the stems, are particularly effective in vertical, rhythmic compositions.

Front or back: Above, one arrangement is photographed from two sides. Notice how the pebble bed is massed about the base of the flowers, and thins out as it approaches the far edge of the bowl.

The flowers here are rearranged in a *low* composition. Here the stems have been trimmed of all but their uppermost levels. With the arrangement made on varying levels, a feeling of movement is still possible.

Iris, if you like them tall...

Iris, like Peruvian lilies and gladioli, make wonderful vertical arrangements. You can often use iris and gladioli interchangeably — whichever is available in your garden or at your florist.

Above, a few iris rise in a single upright line from a bed of pebbles placed to one side of a round low bowl. The needle holder is well anchored with clay.

Iris and carnations are two flowers that florists frequently box together — seldom with enough carnations for a separate arrangement. On the opposite page the iris are placed first, in a verticle radiating pattern. The few carnations face out at the base of the arrangement, the tallest rising to about one-third the height of the tallest iris.

For your entrance hall...

Today's handsome dahlias are mostly descendants of the wild dahlias of Mexico. Here some of the wild natural feeling of this popular flower is recaptured in a simple free arrangement. Notice how the buds swing out on lines of their own, how flowers and foliage keep to separate levels.

For your living room...

This is a composition you can make with a wide variety of flowers. Two main lines rise from one side of a low rectangular bowl, the first sweeping straight up and to the right, the second moving away at a low level, reaching well beyond the left side of the bowl.

This stately arrangement is easy.
Start with the center stalk...

Favorite annual of many northern gardeners, stock is another flower that looks well in tall, stately arrangements. Here six stems are placed in a deep vase, secured with one needle holder.

1. Place the tallest stock first, over-all height three times that of the vase.

2. Working from the top down, place the next stems to support the verticle line.

3. In the finished arrangement, on the opposite page, major blooms are in three levels. Buds have been added on the right for balance.

When you make mixed arrangements...

One general principle in arrangement is particularly useful when you are mixing two different flowers: keep the *larger* blooms at the base, the smaller at the top. In the photograph above, delphiniums rise high above the bowl, tapering off in small nodding buds. Big single gaillardia surround the base of the delphinium stems.

Nature is informal. You can be too..

Informality in flower arrangement sometimes means nothing more than lack of crowding, and freedom of movement. Here the dark gold chrysanthemums establish the outer line, the small white chrysanthemums are spaced naturally (and hence informally) in the center. One large needle holder supports the complete arrangement

You can build almost anything
if you have three needle holders...

You can't have too many needle holders. Often you'll find yourself using two, three or more in a single arrangement to achieve some new effect in color and form. Collect needle holders in different sizes and shapes — and be sure they are heavy.

This arrangement, compact and low in silhouette, is effective in a living room, facing out from any table arranged along a wall. If additional chrysanthemums are placed on the far side, the arrangement will be effective on a dinner table, attractive from all sides.

1. Arrange stalks of yellow coxcomb at three descending levels, establishing the height of the finished arrangement.

2. Add five to eight yellow-centered white chrysanthemums grouped naturally about the stalks of the coxcomb.

3. Complete the arrangement with a few yellow-green leaves such as privet. The leaves, concealing the needle holders, will establish a green base from which the chrysanthemums and coxcomb appear to grow naturally.

Build this from the top down...

Compare this arrangement, using two dozen yellow marguerites, with the coxcomb and chrysanthemum arrangement on the preceding page. It is quite different in appearance, yet the basic plan is the same.

Place three needle holders in line in a low bowl. Start the arrangement at the top, inserting the tallest blooms first. Build down cutting stems shorter and shorter.

This is an arrangement for a low table against a wall; each flower faces upward and outward into the room.

Build this from the center out...

This small arrangement is built around a central group of five yellow-centered white chrysanthemums. One needle holder is placed back-center in an eight-inch square bowl. The three longest-stemmed flowers rise directly from the holder. The fourth bloom faces slightly to the left, the fifth bloom directly left.

A few yellow strawflowers are added on the right to balance the composition. The two stones form a basic part of the arrangement, suggesting the earth — source of the flowers' growth.

The feeling of movement —
a sloop running before the wind...

Stiffness and rigidity have no place in flower arrangement. Freedom and movement are everything.

Imagine your low bowl is the hull of a sloop. There is a good breeze coming in off the stern. Place one tall stem of white stock up front. It is the mast; so curve it a little. Let two or three stems push out in front; they are the jib, bellied in the wind. Fill the space back of the mast with a descending swell of stock, pushing out from the bowl all in one direction.

No one knows it's a sloop — except you. But chances are someone in your house, noticing the flowers, will say, "How natural they look. I can almost see them moving in the wind."

Symmetrical, in a small bowl...

This loosely placed bouquet combines lavender centaurea (a wonderful flower for cutting) with yellow double coreopsis. Notice how you can attain a general feeling of symmetry without stiffness. The centaurea are placed at irregular intervals, introducing their color in splashes.

Exotic, clinging to one large stone...

The large stone sets the theme of this arrangement. Coxcomb hugs its upper peri-meter; a few croton leaves spread themselves as a backdrop.

The arrangement is made in a large fourteen-inch bowl, with three needle holders. A few pebbles break up the line of contact between the large stone and the bowl.

Anywhere you put it, a small
arrangement will brighten a room...

Flowers have a way of relaxing a room, making it look cheerful and lived-in. The kind of flowers isn't very important; the amount isn't important at all

Here are two handsful of sweet peas, just out of the garden. The arrangement is an informal bouquet, made with a wire holder in a small four-inch bowl. A few single flowers are permitted to break away from the mass, with careful placement to avoid an unnatural, too-perfect outline.

Leaves should "grow" naturally from the bowl...

Leaves are pleasant any time; but they are indispensable in the fall and winter, when your garden is out of action and your house desperately needs something fresh indoors.

Here, a single branch, with two sub-branches, is simply placed upright in a shallow dish, anchored with one needle holder. The heavy stones at the base add interest.

Leaves in movement are exciting...

A windblown effect is often easy to achieve with leaves. Use the natural curves of the branches, all in the same direction — not with one offsetting another.

Let the highest branch extend out beyond the dish at one side, then step the branches down in height. A clay-anchored needle holder is usually best for this type of branch arrangement.

Branches in movement...

The illusions of growth, air and movement can be obtained easily with a few branches. Scotch broom, picked after the blossoms have fallen, is used here. Pussy willows are wonderful in the spring, as are plum and cherry branches, or dogwood.

Don't overdo. One or two branches are often enough, if you pick and cut them to rise naturally from the bowl, at varying levels. Use your flower snips to cut away sub-branches that cross over or confuse the simple upward-rising composition.

PHLOX

Flowers in movement...

Color can accentuate the sweep and movement of your arrangements.

The colors above are reddish-pink, lavender and white. The dark values dominate at the left and center, the light values and white on the outside and at the extreme right. The complete arrangement moves in a horizontal line away from the bowl.

Four branches of chrysanthemums...

In late autumn the chrysanthemum comes into its own. Often the last flowers to come indoors from your garden will be a few branches of mums. Make the most of them by displaying stems and leaves as well as flowers.

On the left, four branches rise from a shallow dish to three principal levels, the lowest leaves concealing the supporting needle holder.

Above, the same four branches are placed in a deep pottery vase, longest stems to the right, shortest stems just reaching over the rim of the container.

STOCK

White Stock, arranged with gladioli...

It's fun to experiment with color, to paint your own color compositions. And it's easy if your medium is flowers and not paint.

Here is a simple color composition made with gladioli and white stock. The stock is arranged first, from the center of the bowl. The glads form an irregular band of brilliant yellow about the base.

Petunias with gladioli...

This time give the glads their usual height, one above another, in a single, vertical line. Then place pink petunias in a sweeping mass at the base and up to the right. The colors, deliberately separated, contribute to the movement and interest of the complete arrangement.

Try placing just three flowers
in a free arrangement...

An arrangement made with three flowers is unquestionably more difficult than most arrangements made with a dozen. But such an extremely simple flower plan offers the best of practice, a chance to try out fundamentals, a chance to prove to yourself that numbers are far less important than technique and your own creative skill.

Here three marguerites rise at traditional levels, all flowers reaching above the upper limit of the foliage. A long flat dish, six by eight inches, is used with a round needle holder.

Glads against a wall...

Above, a dozen gladioli are arranged in symmetrical balance, vertically. Place five to six tall glads at the back; then step down in front, cutting stems shorter and shorter until the last flowers cover the two needle holders. Place leaves carefully behind and between the flowers.

On the right, seven or eight gladioli combine in a diagonal arrangement. The flowers rise in a column to the left, balanced by leaves. The bowl is nine inches square. Two needle holders support the arrangement.

| MARIGOLDS |

Don't snub marigolds. They are
getting handsomer all the time...

Here is a Cinderella flower with all the homely virtues — inexpensive in the shops, easy to grow in your own garden, blooming steadily until late autumn, sturdy and long-lasting after cutting.

Now marigolds are appearing in new varieties — golden yellow to maroon-red in color, odorless if you wish, as beautiful as they are useful.

On the left, a dozen yellow and maroon marigolds are arranged in informal vertical balance: flowers to the right, greens massed to the left.

Above, maroon marigolds combine with yellow and orange-red strawflowers and statice in an informal bouquet. Marigold buds are placed to emphasize the left-balance of the arrangement.

Try phlox in combinations...

Simple white phlox combines well with many of the showier varieties. *Above,* white phlox is arranged with deep purple and lavender phlox. The flowers are massed close to the bowl, dark colors to the right and left, with a few, delicate, light-colored sprays rising above.

Lavender phlox and yellow marguerites are arranged together. Notice how the yellow flowers are held toward the center, with the darker colors around the outer edge. A few flowers on the right break away from the central arrangement.

A spray arrangement for a
small dinner party...

Here is a conventional dinner arrangement that escapes being commonplace by the way you handle the cutting and placement of the individual flowers.

Two sprays of snapdragons sweep out from the glass bowl, one almost reaching down to the table runner. Without disturbing the arrangement's basic symmetry, the sprays pick everything up with a sense of natural movement.

Establish the position and length of the sprays at the very start – also the height of the arrangement.

Fill in the outline; then move the two long sprays into their final positions, each at its own level.

FUCHSIA and
CHRYSANTHEMUM

Convertible arrangements,
two different examples...

Above is a casual arrangement which recaptures, indoors, a natural branch and leaf order originally observed in the woods. It doesn't matter that the original was a weed clump, and this indoor composition fuchsia. The plan's the thing — you can execute it in whatever materials are suitable and handy. The primary line rises high to the right, the secondary line low and to the left. The tertiary line is minimized — just two low branches, one on each side.

On the right, another "convertible" arrangement — this time with chrysanthemums, though equally effective with carnations, dahlias, zinnias, petunias or most other medium-sized flowers. Compare it with the Shasta Daisy arrangement on page 33. The flower order here is 3-3-4-2; yet the effect is much the same, a free composition with no two flowers on quite the same level.

GAILLARDIA

Try for effects of your own..

The two arrangements on these pages are both examples of free interpretation of the "three levels" principle. *Above,* the top and second levels are sufficiently established with two pairs of flowers. *On the right,* four flowers establish the mid-level, but a dozen or so are used below and eight or nine above, with buds weaving their way informally at every level.

CHRYSANTHEMUMS

This book has contained no rules, because rules imply rigidity, and flower arrangements should be free, unrestricted. There has been, however, quite a lot of discussion of the *general principles* of good flower arrangement. Remember, none of these principles should be considered as a hard and fast guide to be followed always. Instead, try to approach flowers as freely as you can, understanding the principles, using them most of the time, but disregarding them whenever they get in your way. The composition is important, not the theory behind it.

Alphabetical List of
Flowers Included in Arrangements